WRITE NOW!

WRITE NOW!
Literacy Through Creative Writing Craft

Dr Shelley Davidow & Dr Paul Williams

Published in 2025 by Amba Press, Melbourne, Australia
www.ambapress.com.au

© Shelley Davidow and Paul Williams 2025

All rights reserved. No part of this book may be reproduced or transmitted in any form or by any means, electronic or mechanical, including photocopying, recording or by any information storage and retrieval system, without prior permission in writing from the publisher.

Cover design: Tess McCabe
Internal design: Amba Press
Editor: Rica Dearman

ISBN: 9781923215542 (pbk)
ISBN: 9781923215559 (ebk)

A catalogue record for this book is available from the National Library of Australia.

CONTENTS

About the authors   1
Introduction   3
What's in this book and how to use it   5
Curriculum overview   9

Part A: Playing with words   13

Introduction to this section   15
Lesson 1	Words	17
Lesson 2	Sentences	25
Lesson 3	Sound	33
Lesson 4	Whose point of view?	41
Lesson 5	Imagery	49
Lesson 6	Setting	55
Lesson 7	Characters	61
Lesson 8	Purple prose	69
Lesson 9	Plot and the narrative arc	75
Lesson 10	Innovation and experimentation	81

Part B: The hero's journey — 89

Introduction to this section		91
Lesson 11	Finding a hero	93
Lesson 12	(Almost) every story is a hero's journey	99
Lesson 13	The road ahead...	103
Lesson 14	The beginning of the hero's journey	107
Lesson 15	On the journey – fun and games	111
Lesson 16	The ending – all is (not) lost	115
Lesson 17	Editing the story	119
Lesson 18	Peer editing	125
Lesson 19	Final edit	129
Lesson 20	In-class showcase	131
References		137
Note on rubrics and assessment of creative writing		141
Appendix A	Portfolio marking template – self-review	143
Appendix B	Portfolio marking template – educator	145
Appendix C	Story marking template	147
Appendix D	Young authors' response to the program	151

ABOUT THE AUTHORS

Dr Shelley Davidow is an award-winning international author who grew up in South Africa. Writing across genres, her fifty books reflect her experiences living and working on five continents over two decades. Recent publications include the novel *The Girl with the Violin* (HarperCollins, 2024), the parenting book *Grounded* (Amba Press, 2024) and the memoirs *Runaways* (Ultimo, 2022), *Shadow Sisters* (University of Queensland Press, 2018) and *Whisperings in the Blood* (University of Queensland Press, 2016).

For twenty years, Shelley was a school teacher in the United States and in Australia, teaching every age from Kindergarten through to Year 12. Her current day job is Senior Lecturer in Education at the University of the Sunshine Coast in Queensland. She's also a facilitator in Restorative Practice and consults with schools and communities around the country. In the time that's left over, she runs creative writing workshops and is also a HeartMath Coach and Mentor. She lives near a saltwater lake with her family and some tame kookaburras.

Dr Paul Williams grew up in Zimbabwe and has lived on five continents. He has published internationally across several genres: crime fiction, young adult fantasy and mystery, memoir, non-fiction, short stories and critical articles. His first writing projects sold more than two hundred thousand copies in South Africa,

Zimbabwe, Kenya and Swaziland. His memoir *Soldier Blue* (David Philip Publishers, 2008) won Book of the Year in South Africa in 2008, and *The Secret of Old Mukiwa* (College Press, 2000) won Best Young Adult fiction at the International African Book Fair in 2001. His novels include *Don't Tell* (Bloodhound Books, 2020), *Twelve Days* (Bloodhound Books, 2019), *Cokcraco* (Lacuna, 2013) and *Parallax* (Zharmae, 2014). He is currently Associate Professor and Discipline Lead of Creative Industries in the School of Business and Creative Industries at the University of the Sunshine Coast in Queensland.

INTRODUCTION

Welcome to *Write Now!* – a resource for educators and their writers – packed with sequential, progressive and inspiring writing exercises for all ages.

In this book, we share our approach to teaching literacy through creative writing. Our combined half a century of writing, publishing, editing and teaching experience will hopefully inspire the next generation of young writers to use their words well, to find their unique voices, and to be able to write whatever they would like to write. We know what destroys the love of words and writing, and also what ignites it. Everything in this book is designed to ignite it.

As well as our fiction and non-fiction published across multiple genres, we've written several international books on creative writing: *Playing with Words: An Introduction to Creative Writing Craft* (Bloomsbury, 2016), *Novel Ideas* (Red Globe Press, 2019) and *Writing the Radical Memoir* (Bloomsbury, 2022). Our research on which the rubric at the end is based, is published in our article 'Re-imagining narrative writing and assessment' in *The Australian Journal of Language and Literacy* in 2022

Also, a quick heads-up: this is not NAPLAN preparation, nor ACARA curriculum preparation. The book may check ACARA language and literacy boxes, but that's not our aim. The focus is to inspire young people to love writing and write well. That's it.

Our research indicates that after completing the lessons in this book, young writers will improve (Carey et al., 2022). Through a series of fun, imaginative, craft-focused exercises spread out over twenty lessons, young writers will be given the chance to explore their own power with words and to learn new skills that are ultimately transferable to every subject area where writing is required. Of course, there is already a body of research indicating that teaching creative writing is an effective strategy to improve literacy (Isbell et al, 2004; Mello, 2001; Eder, 2007; Wallace, 2000; Cliatt & Shaw, 1988; Miller & Pennycuff, 2008). Sometimes it is challenging to teach the craft of writing if educators themselves don't feel confident. It's our aim to support educators to approach writing as an art, a craft and a skill, much like sculpting, or visual arts or music.

We love words. We want young writers to have the tools to write anything and to love words, too. Each individual deserves the space in which to find their voices and express their thoughts. We hope this book provides that space. As the adults who will be teaching the next generation of young writers, we hope educators, too, will find joy in the process, and sometimes join in and experience writing together as a collective and community-building act.

WHAT'S IN THIS BOOK AND HOW TO USE IT

There are twenty full sessions/lessons in *Write Now!* Each one should take 60-90 minutes. The lessons can be spread out over a year when time allows, or if a curriculum is more flexible, everything can be covered in twenty weeks. The focus is on building writing capacity progressively.

Freewriting/writing 'white hot'

Each lesson commences with a 'two-minute freewrite'. Freewriting is a method of writing that increases the flow of ideas and blocks the inner censor or editor, any critical voice that might stifle spontaneity (Elbow, 1973). Freewriting may also help to increase fluency in those young writers who have difficulty writing. The fear of failure can impair creative thought and action, sometimes resulting in procrastination or avoidance. Freewriting is designed to bypass the inner critic, editor and 'grammar police'. It is the realm of dreams, myths, metaphors and random ideas.

The time limit allows for a burst of creative energy that does not go on beyond two minutes. Another word for freewriting is what John Braine calls 'white hot writing' (Braine, 1975, p.21), which is a technique to help writers get words on a page as fast as possible before doubts about writing ability or writer's block set in. Young writers can be inspired by the knowledge that all good books and pieces of writing go through this first stage of writing before they are edited and polished. Imaginations are the furnaces in which ideas are born. First drafts and freewrites need to flow without fear of what ought to be written.

It is recommended that the educator do some of the activities alongside young writers – sometimes revealing their work, too. This creates a shared experience and establishes everyone as a writer in their own right. We'd like to give a nod to our bestselling creative writing handbook for adult writers *Playing with Words: An Introduction to Creative Writing Craft* (Bloomsbury, 2016). Some of the exercises in this book are drawn from more sophisticated versions first published in that work.

Reading/sharing

After each exercise in each session, we suggest that three or four yong writers are invited to share their work. Over time, we've found that those who might be hesitant to read their work at first, gain confidence when they see that the space is about playfulness and exploration, not judgement. Reading aloud is always a good idea. It helps writers and listeners to hear the music, the cadence, the 'voice' and tone of the writer. And, of course, reading aloud is associated with improved reading fluency, pronunciation and prosody (Beers, 2003; Gibson, 2008; Goodwin & Redfern, 2000).

At the end of each exercise, if volunteers are hesitant to share what they've written, we've found this question helpful:

> *Did anyone write something that was completely unexpected, that kind of just fell into your head from nowhere?*

Editing

Editing strategies covered in this book include: 1) Planning; 2) Drafting; 3) Revising; 4) Proofreading; and 5) Publishing – but this happens for the most part in Part B and relies on the fact the young writers will have had plenty of opportunity to learn the art and craft of playing with words in different ways first.

Assessment

In the appendix we've provided rubrics for self, peer and teacher assessment based on the skills and capacities developed over the lessons. The rubrics are the result of the study we undertook with young writers (Carey et al., 2022), which demonstrated how teaching creative writing craft in schools improves overall literacy. We have amended the rubrics slightly to make them fit for purpose and easily usable by anyone reading this book.

Publication

We encourage educators to consider collecting student work into a published class/group anthology and having a book launch/reading event at the end of the course. In our experience this has been a phenomenal success, providing young writers with tangible, real-world experience of the journey from creative process to final product. We provide the 'how to publish' and 'how to organise a launch' at the end of the book.

Also, starting out with the goal and expectation of publication is likely to increase engagement and commitment. The real-world output of the young writer's creative work validates the process, employs cross-curricular skills, and creates a valuable platform for 'expression'.

The book launch allows the school to acknowledge, highlight and display respect and acceptance of the authors' identity that the young writers share.

Consider the logistics of the publishing activities before starting the program to ensure they are achievable.

Imaginative capacities

This book places a high value on supporting the development of 'imaginative capacities'. While the Australian curriculum refers to 'creative thinking' in an attempt to capture these capacities, we feel it does not go far enough to demonstrate exactly how 'young writers learn... to generate and apply new ideas in specific contexts... [involving] complex representations and images' (Australian Curriculum, 2021). Bloom's taxonomy defines such capacities as 'putting elements together to form a coherent or functional whole; reorganizing elements into a new pattern or structure through generating, planning or producing' (Anderson & Krathwohl 2001, p.21). Again, we think this doesn't go far enough in capturing exactly what imaginative capacities are. Franklin and Theall in 'Developing Creative Capacities' (2021) suggest that such capacities are qualities of subjects (creative writers and thinkers) rather than specific applied techniques, and these capacities include 'strong motivation, endurance, intellectual curiosity, independence in thought and action, strong desire for self-realization, strong sense of self, etc.' (Brolin 1992).

Well, that perhaps gives the academic underpinnings of some of the capacities we hope to pass on to young writers. We hope they will develop the confidence in their own ability to distil their imaginations, thoughts and insights into words.

Enjoy the journey – start Write Now!

Shelley and Paul

CURRICULUM OVERVIEW

Overall learning outcomes

By the end of this course, young writers will be able to:

- Engage with words to develop a sense of individual voice
- Recognise techniques and approaches in their own and others' work
- Play with techniques and approaches to generate inspiration and ideas
- Understand through writing practice how their craft enables an artistic end product
- Develop a variety of forms, techniques and writing styles
- Evaluate the works of peer writers – and any literary work
- Develop transferable literacy capacity to improve communication in a variety of contexts

Some content description alignments with ACARA exist, since the book builds capacity in:

- Literacy
- Critical and creative thinking
- Personal and social capability
- Ethical understanding

Language

Specifically, young writers will:

- Understand the way language evolves to reflect a changing world
- Understand the use of punctuation to support meaning
- Express and develop ideas
- Analyse how point of view is generated

Literature

Specifically, young writers will:

- Compare the ways that language is used to create character and to influence emotions and opinions in different types of texts
- Reflect on ideas and opinions about characters, settings and events in literary texts
- Discuss aspects of texts, for example, their aesthetic and social value
- Identify and discuss main ideas, concepts and points of view in spoken texts to evaluate qualities
- Use interaction skills when discussing and presenting ideas and information

Literacy

Young writers will be able to:

- Analyse and explain the ways text structures and language features shape meaning and vary according to audience and purpose

Creating texts

Young writers will also be able to:

- Plan, draft and publish imaginative texts
- Edit for meaning
- Use a range of software, including word-processing programs, to confidently create, edit and publish

But these are the by-products of an exciting, inspiring white-hot creative writing process, not the end goal.

Part A: Write Now

The first ten lessons – summarised in Table 1 below – are adaptations of some of the most useful creative writing exercises in the authors' bestselling university level adult writers handbook *Playing with Words: An Introduction to Creative Writing Craft* (Bloomsbury, 2016). The aim is to inspire young writers to play with words as they might play with paint on a canvas. There is an emphasis on the creative, imaginative aspect of writing; young writers are encouraged to experiment without fear of failure.

Table 1: Overview of the ten *Write Now!* lessons

Part A: Playing with words	
1	**Words:** playing with form and word associations; poetry exercises
2	**Sentences and paragraphs:** short and long sentences; the rules and when to break them; playful sentence exercises
3	**Sound:** rhythm and your unique voice; the punctuation police; rap; alliteration; assonance

4	**Point of view:** who's telling the story; first, second and third person; unreliable and omniscient narrators; in tense writing: tenses – past, present and future
5	**Imagery:** painting the picture through similes, metaphors, symbols and figurative speech; using the five senses
6	**Setting:** landscapes, internal and external; movie angles; showing not telling
7	**Characters:** dialogue; being in other people's shoes
8	**Purple prose:** overwriting; melodrama
9	**Plot:** the narrative arc
10	**Innovation and experimentation:** crazy experiments that won't blow anything up

PART A

Playing with words

INTRODUCTION TO THIS SECTION

Each lesson begins with a freewrite, followed by several exercises, which will encourage young writers to explore different aspects of craft. It's good if young writers are made aware that these 'white-hot' first drafts are raw, unedited expressions and that the creating/making process is separate to the editing process which will come later. Allow three or four young writers to share their work after each exercise. Over the course of a few weeks, everyone will get a chance to be heard – if they wish.

LESSON 1
WORDS

Aim: The objective of this lesson is to engage young writers and rekindle a love of words and language.

Learning outcomes: By the end of this lesson, young writers will be able to:

- Generate ideas
- Play with new forms

Exercise 1: Freewrite

One of the biggest challenges people have when they begin to write is trying to write something perfect or important straight away. A freewrite is a way to let the brain run wild with ideas without letting the inner critic get in the way.

 Freewrite

Write for two minutes without stopping. Don't worry about spelling, grammar or punctuation. If anyone wants to read their freewrite aloud afterwards, they can, but there's no obligation to do so.

Begin with: 'I've never told you this about me before, but…'

Exercise 2: Beautiful random poems

In this exercise, the focus is on enjoying words and freeing up the process of generating ideas. This exercise encourages random association by pairing two previously unassociated words. The results may be surprising!

Everyone gets to play with words and then use random associations to inspire a poem.

 Beautiful random poems

Write down four nouns one under the other. For example:

Flower
Jacket
Lion
Drain

Now, write four nouns next to the ones you just wrote down. For example:

Flower   Phone
Jacket   Painting
Lion   Hope
Drain   Cloud

Now, draw random lines from any word on the left to any word on the right. For example:

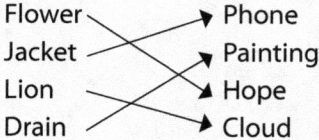

Choose one pair. For example: Lion Cloud. This is now the title of your poem! You have six minutes to write a short poem underneath your new title. It does not have to rhyme. Afterwards, up to four people can share their work.

Here is an example by Shelley Davidow:

Cloud Lion

At condensation point
Above my head
Blown by wind
He starts to grow
White on blue
First a head
Then an eye
Then a wild mane
His mouth opens to roar
And for a moment –
Perfection:
My white cloud-lion against the endless blue.
His roar breaks him apart.
The wind blows through him
Dissolves him
His moment
Evaporates.

Exercise 3: Free verse poetry with prompt

In this exercise, inspiration is drawn from a William Carlos Williams poem, 'The Red Wheelbarrow'. The poem is the foundation for young writers to write their own poem using the same beginning, 'So much depends upon…' The idea is to work with an example as a template and have the freedom to play, using their own ideas. If the result is not a strict copy of the form, it doesn't matter. The main idea is that the poem and first line act as a prompt. Young writers should be encouraged to see how a simple sentence can become a poem, how line breaks are made in certain places, allowing the reader's focus to fall on the end words and the beginning words.

'The Red Wheelbarrow' exercise

Write a poem in five minutes, starting with the same words, 'So much depends upon…' and try to follow the format of the original by using the words in bold in your own poem (don't worry if you do things a bit differently). See the authors' attempt after the original.

'The Red Wheelbarrow' by William Carlos Williams
so much depends
upon

a red wheel
barrow

glazed with rain
water

beside the white
chickens

'Hot Chocolate' by Shelley Davidow and Paul Williams
so much depends
upon

a cup
of hot chocolate

topped with
marshmallows

upon the wooden
table

Exercise 4: Concrete poetry

Concrete poetry is poetry where the poem looks like the thing it is representing. It can rhyme or not. The objective is to have fun making the words into pictures, and being imaginative and playful.

 Concrete poetry exercise

Write a concrete poem – where the poem looks like the thing that it is about – alone or with a partner. For example, write a car poem that looks like a car or a poem about a leaf falling that looks like a leaf falling. Be inventive, like the example below:

Dorthi Charles (b. 1963)
Concrete Cat (1971)

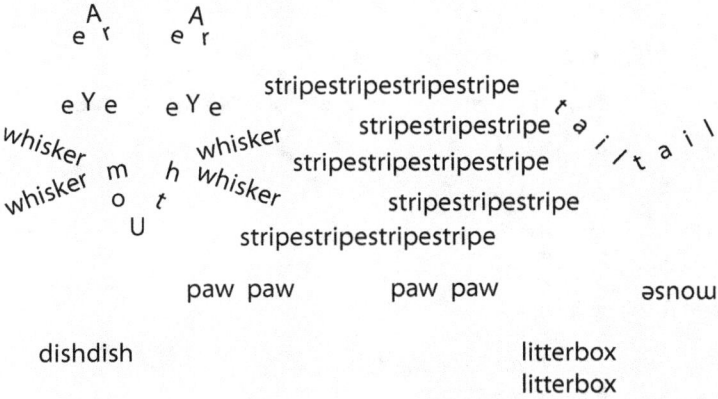

Write a few more if time allows.

Other examples can be found by searching for 'concrete poetry' online.

Exercise 5: Limericks

A limerick is a humorous poem consisting of five lines. The strict but simple rhyme scheme and the strong rhythm pattern allows for a unique and often hilarious outcome. Young writers will be challenged to search for the right words, find the right rhythm and come to a sometimes outlandish conclusion. Though it's important to count the syllables – as the rhythm depends on an exact number of syllables per line, and follow the rhyme scheme so that the words at the end of specific lines have the same end sounds – having a go is much more important than writing the 'perfect' limerick.

A limerick has five lines. Lines one, two and five rhyme with each other, and lines three and four rhyme with each other. The rhythm is eight syllables in the first, second and fifth lines, and five in the third and fourth.

 Limerick exercise

Using the example below, write a limerick or two (or three!)

Line 1 = 8 syllables A
Line 2 = 8 syllables A
Line 3 = 5 syllables B
Line 4 = 5 or 6 syllables B
Line 5 = 8 syllables A

There once was a woman called Dot
Who was an incredible clot!
She swallowed a slug
On the side of her mug
And it stuck in her throat like snot! (Ugh!)

Verbal reflection/discussion

What did you enjoy the most in this lesson?

....

....

....

....

What did you find the most challenging?

....

....

....

....

What new insight or thought about writing did you gain today?

....

....

....

....

Anything else?

....

....

....

....

LESSON 2
SENTENCES

Aim: This lesson is designed to engage young writers in building and understanding sentences – what some of the rules are, and how to break them for effect.

Learning outcomes: By the end of this lesson, young writers will be able to:

- Play with sentence structure to generate inspiration and ideas
- Understand the power of using short and long sentences, and how to use sentence fragments and run-ons deliberately and for effect

Introduction to lesson

It's important that young writers understand that the purpose of a good sentence is to get the reader to the next one – and after that, to build a powerful paragraph. And then – they need to know that the purpose of a paragraph is to get the reader to the next one. Young writers need to see that the purpose of learning grammar is not some tortuous meaningless exercise, but that knowing at least some of the rules (and how to break them) gives them more control and power over a narrative.

A few things about sentences: our definition is that a simple sentence has at least a subject and a verb – that means that *someone* or *something does* or *has something*.

Jacob swims.
(subject + verb)

Also, long and short sentences create different rhythms. Young writers can discover for themselves (AFTER doing the relevant exercises), what the impact of using a short sentence is. Does it create tension or maybe drama, for example? Maybe they discover that long sentences lend themselves to inner dialogue, thoughts or memory recall?

The exercises look at so-called sentence errors such as fragments and run-ons. When these are used purposely and for effect, young writers can see for themselves what happens when fragments without verbs are used – or what the effect of a run-on sentence, which lacks commas, full stops and other punctuation, might be.

Working consciously with run-ons and fragments is likely to reduce the inadvertent and less effective use of these.

Exercise 1: Freewrite

 Freewrite

Write for two minutes without stopping. Don't worry about spelling, grammar or punctuation. If anyone wants to read their freewrite afterwards, they can, but there's no obligation to do so.

Begin with: 'I opened the box with a racing heart…'

Exercise 2: The longest sentence in the world

Are these sentences? *I am. It is. Both are.* All three are, actually. They all contain the necessary ingredients for a complete sentence: they each have a subject and a verb, but they are very simple sentences and can be expanded.

 The longest sentence in the world exercise

Create a long sentence in the next five minutes. Start with a simple sentence and build on it by inserting clauses between commas. Use the same structure in the examples below to build your sentence:

Step 1: The man went for a walk. (Someone does something)

Step 2: The man went for a walk with his dog. (Someone does something with someone or something)

Step 3: The man, who had short, blond, wild, uncombed hair went for a walk with his dog which was a magic animal. (Now we describe the man and his dog)

Step 4: The man, who had short, blond, wild, uncombed hair went for a walk with his dog which was a magic animal and which he had stolen from a circus many years ago.

Step 5: Any ideas on how to make the sentence even longer?

Exercise 3: Short, sharp sentences

A sentence can be as short as 'I am', as long as it has a subject and a verb (or even an implied subject, such as 'Go!'). Short sentences in a paragraph speed up the pace of what's happening and can be used to generate excitement or tension.

Short, sharp sentences exercise

Write a creative piece called 'A noise in the night' in 7–10 minutes. Use very short sentences of ten words or less, like the example below:

The tower stood on the hill. The dark city lay beneath. His heart raced. His fingers clung to the concrete edge. His legs dangled against the wall. The wind blew hard and cold. His arms ached. He looked down from the top. It was a long way down. Beneath him, he saw the moon in the river. He began to lose his grip, when suddenly, a sound tore through the air.

Exercise 4: Long, languorous sentences

Using long, languorous sentences allows for a character to have an inner life – to consider and remember and wonder. Encourage young writers to imagine what a character might be thinking about on a long train journey to a welcome or an unwelcome destination.

 Long, languorous sentences exercise

Write for 7–10 minutes about a long journey to an unwelcome destination. Allow the thoughts of the character on this journey to wander. Where is this person coming from? Where are they going? Why? Use long sentences like in the example below:

The countryside is covered in mist and low clouds hang over the mountain as the train clatters its way through low visibility away from my parents who have once again been sent on a secret mission. The last time I saw Aunt Dora, I was about three, and even then I didn't especially like her. She was a short, hard-faced woman who wore sickly floral perfume, and she used to squeeze my cheeks until they hurt as she exclaimed, "She is so cute, isn't she? So cute!" I really wasn't looking forward to spending the whole of my summer holidays trapped in her big old creepy house with only her dog Fergus for a friend, while the rest of my friends headed to the beach with their families...

Exercise 5: The long and short of it

Using both short and long sentences together and on purpose allows for energetic writing. Readers will be compelled to keep reading when the pace and tension of the writing is engaging. Hopefully, it's evident that short sentences can be used to create tension, while long ones give the reader a chance to experience someone's interior thoughts. In the next exercise, young writers get to put both together for a powerful, punchy paragraph.

 The long and short of it exercise

Imagine a character, walking down the road. Something unexpected happens. This event could be terrifying, funny or exciting. Write for 7–10 minutes and use long and short sentences like in the example below:

I dashed into the woods. My legs shook. I stopped to catch my breath. I was about to continue running on the path when I heard it behind me – that strange sound I'd been running from. It sounded like a whine or a howl. I listened again. I heard nothing. Then, suddenly, a crash of branches startled me. What was that? A wolf? Something grey leapt out of the bushes and snarled at me, its jaws wide open, its fangs showing. It couldn't be real! I ran as fast as I could out of the woods and did not stop running until

I was back on the road, wondering if this was something real or whether I'd only imagined it because I was frightened and my mind was possibly playing tricks on me. At the road, I stopped. I looked back and saw nothing, but then, from the woods came a sound that made me shiver all over – the sound of a long, ear-splitting howl.

Exercise 6: Freaky fragments

Sentence fragments are what they sound like – fragments. This means they have either no subject or no verb. There are style guides and standardised testing guides that maintain these are incorrect, but real authors all over the world use them all the time – on purpose and for effect. A sentence fragment doesn't make sense on its own and isn't complete, but used carefully in a paragraph, it can have a powerful effect. For those who need to know, a sentence fragment is defined as a dependent clause belonging to a missing main sentence, such as: The road shimmering. Or: While I was swimming.

 Freaky fragments exercise

Write a paragraph of about 50–100 words made up only of fragments.

Here's an example:

Late afternoon walk. The gate up head. Creak! The metal cold as he touches it. Opening the gate. The sound of the bull in the paddock snorting. Tiptoeing. Don't breathe. The crack of a twig. The bull turning its head. Red eyes. An animal lowering its horns. Run!

Exercise 7: Roller-coaster run-ons

Runs-ons are sentences without the so-called relevant punctuation called 'run-ons', not because they are necessarily long, but because they lack punctuation which is not given here in our example on purpose, so we can show and not just tell readers how run-ons can create a sense of breathlessness and urgency, and how they might be appropriate for certain subject matter and not others.

Roller-coaster run-ons exercise
Write a paragraph about something urgent without punctuation so the sentence goes on and on. Read the following example paragraph, then write one. Have fun!

I am roller-skating down the hill faster and faster no brakes I jam my foot on the stop harder harder but no nothing works the speed is crazy must be edging up to 40 50 60 kilometers an hour and I struggle to hold myself upright the wheel turning pulling grating against the road help help what can I do the houses whiz by then I realise it's deliberate someone has messed with my brakes someone wants me dead too late too late my life flashes by no the road flashes by faster faster I'm not going to make it around the next bend I hit the barrier and crash through and I'm cascading down and plummeting towards the ground I close my eyes wait for the impact the last thing I see is her face.

Extension exercise
Write a paragraph using the freewrite from this lesson, the short and long sentences exercise and the fragments and/or run-ons to create a short narrative.

Verbal reflection/discussion

What did you enjoy the most in this lesson?

What did you find the most challenging?

What new insight or thought about writing did you gain today?

Anything else?

LESSON 3
SOUND

Aim: The goal of this lesson is to engage young writers in building 'voice' through craft-focused exercises.

Learning outcomes: By the end of this lesson, young writers will be able to:

- Understand how rhythm, repetition and grammar choices create 'voice'

Introduction to lesson

What is voice? When writers speak of 'finding their voice' or readers say they like 'the voice' in a story, what does that really mean? A singer can have a great voice, but a writer's voice is like a watermark. It is the blueprint of the author, the choice of words, the rhythm, the repetition, the grammar, the overall sense of how the narrative is told.

How do young writers learn to find their voice/s? (A single writer can have as many voices as there are stories to be told, by the way!) The answers may be found in the exercises that follow.

Creating voice is like creating identity. Finding a unique voice and style is an empowering and liberating experience. It should be obvious, though, that a young adult novel would have a different voice to a non-fiction guide on oceans, or a spoken word poem. Young writers should be encouraged to create many unique voices by playing and writing within different genres and inhabiting different personas/narrators. The more adept writers become, the more adaptable they are when writing in any genre.

Exercise 1: Freewrite

 Freewrite

Write for two minutes without stopping. Don't worry about spelling, grammar or punctuation. If anyone wants to read their freewrite afterwards, they can, but there's no obligation to do so.

Begin with: 'That morning, the sun rose on a world so strange, I could not believe it…'

Exercise 2: Finding your voice

 Finding your voice exercise

Write a paragraph of 100–200 words and choose a style that fits a particular character. Is the character from another time? Do they use a lot of slang? Are they a teen? A grandmother? A dog? The writer's voice is the result of how language is used. Are there repetitions? Does a person say 'hey' at the end of every sentence? Is the voice sarcastic, loving or angry? Voice can reveal character and relationship.

Here's an example:

It's like, she'd be the little kid who says she's your best friend, but given a chocolate to share with you, if you weren't watching, she'd just eat the whole thing by herself. She's, like, super friendly on the outside and you want to trust her and like her, but then, like, I've seen her do things, like, say things behind people's backs and then be totally friendly to them straight after – and it's like, if she's doing that with them, she's probably one hundred per cent doing that with me, too.

Exercise 3: Having an attitude

'Attitude' in writing is part of what shapes a writing voice. It is often driven by an underlying emotion that isn't named, but can be detected by the reader or listener.

 Attitude of gratitude exercise

Write a paragraph (70–100 words) with one of the following attitudes: the voice could be gushing, clueless, cruel, sarcastic, angry, overbearing, passionate or distrustful. Choose an attitude, but do not explain what it is – just show it. If you share your writing afterwards, listeners may like to have a guess which attitude writers are attempting to show.

Here are some examples:

I'm sure you do really want to know how I am. Yeah. I can see it in your eyes, the casual way you look over my head, the way you just checked your phone in the middle of my answer. I can feel your concern and interest – yeah, thanks a lot. (Attitude: sarcasm)

Oh wow, he looked so cool! I just absolutely loved that style on him, and his shoes, wow, they were so awesome – they just couldn't look better on anyone else – he was like a superstar riding a wave, the way he used his skateboard that afternoon. (Attitude: gushing)

SOUND 35

Exercise 4: Repetition

Repetition of a word, phrase or even a whole line or sentence helps create voice. Repetition creates a certain rhythm as the word or line is foregrounded and highlighted. This also means the weight of the meaning of the written piece lies in the repeated word or phrase. Repetition can be used to great effect to show attitudes like love, humour, irony and even grief.

 Repetition exercise

Write a paragraph that includes a repeated word or phrase.

Here's an example:

I love coffee. I have always loved coffee. I would not survive without coffee. Iced coffee, black coffee, white coffee, three-day-old coffee – any coffee will do. If I don't get my morning double shot, I am a goner. I love coffee. COFFEE 4 E.V.A.

Exercise 5: Healing haikus

Haiku is a Japanese poetic form with specific attributes based on the first ones developed by Matsuo (Master) Bashō (1644–1694). The focus of the subject matter is usually nature, love or life philosophy, or all of those combined in the simple form. In the haiku, the focus is on the sound and rhythm of words, and for that, writers need to count syllables. Simply put, a syllable is a single vowel sound that has one beat. For example, 'hat' has one syllable. 'Syllable' has three syllables: syl-la-ble. 'Happy' has two. A haiku has the following characteristics:

1. 17 total syllables
2. 3 lines of 5-7-5 syllables (or breaths)

3. 2 simple subjects are often placed in juxtaposition, often separated by punctuation; the first part is the set-up, the second part the 'punchline'
4. A keen or unusual observation is made by comparing the two subjects
5. Often contains a seasonal reference about the natural world: 5-7-5

The aim is to use words to create an effect – a rhythm, surprise, voice.

 Healing haiku exercise

Write a haiku about something found in nature, like a frog, spider, thunderstorm or river. Use Bashō's examples below as inspiration:

1. 17 total syllables
2. 3 lines of 5-7-5 syllables (or breaths)
3. The ending should be a surprise or conclusion or ending: 5-7-5

Example 1:

Green and speckled legs,
Hop on logs and lily pads
Splash in cool water.

Example 2:

Blue and turquoise clouds
Travelling with the late wind
Reflect in the lake

Exercise 6: Perfect punctuation

Punctuation works like stage directions in a drama. It's there to create pace, rhythm, tone – and it does matter! The comma, semicolon, colon, dash and ellipses are all tools that have an effect. Importantly, punctuation also changes the meaning of sentences. Young writers will be interested to see how a comma can make all the difference. For example, 'Let's eat Grandma!' is very different from 'Let's eat, Grandma!'

Perfect punctuation exercise

Write a sentence without punctuation. Then rewrite it twice adding punctuation in different ways to give it a different tone and voice. Afterwards, read the sentences dramatically for effect.

Here are some examples:

He walked into the forest there he found a knife a knife.
(No punctuation)

He walked into the forest. There, he found a knife. A knife!

He walked into… the forest. There he found – a knife. A knife?

He walked. Into the forest. There, he found a… knife… a knife?

Extension exercise

Write a 300-word piece weaving together all the exercises in the lesson.

Verbal reflection/discussion

What did you enjoy the most in this lesson?

....
....
....
....

What did you find the most challenging?

....
....
....
....

What new insight or thought about writing did you gain today?

....
....
....
....

Anything else?

....
....
....
....

LESSON 4
WHOSE POINT OF VIEW?

Aim: This lesson seeks to engage young writers in understanding the purpose of, and creating point of view in narrative through a variety of craft-based exercises.

Learning outcomes: By the end of this lesson, young writers will be able to:

- Understand the difference between first, second and third person points of view
- Understand the difference between the omniscient narrator and the close third person
- Use different viewpoints and narrative positions in different pieces for a desired effect

Introduction to lesson

Every story is told from a different perspective. The first thing any reader wants to know is, who is telling the story? Point of view is about the position of the narrator, the one telling the story.

A first person point of view allows the reader to be inside a character's head, which is great, but the limitations are that the reader can't then jump out into someone else's thoughts and know what they are thinking. Also, first person narrators can't have an objective view of themselves without sounding obnoxious. Imagine writing: *My long, brown hair caught the late afternoon sunlight and looked beautiful*; or: *I walked out of the surf, and the sun caught the droplets on my tanned shoulder, highlighting my toned torso.* For that level of observation, the third person omniscient (all-knowing) narrator would have to be used.

But in real life, all we have is our first person point of view. We can only see the world from individual points of view, and cannot get into others' heads to know what they are thinking unless they tell us, or we observe their behaviour.

A third person perspective allows writers to have those observations about their main character – and an omniscient third person narrator allows the reader to see things from different people's perspectives. For example: 'He was an only child and he enjoyed the perks. His mother had made a point of ensuring he got everything she was denied. This was her life's goal.'

A second person perspective is not often found in literature, but it can be very effective. It grabs the reader by the throat and forces them to become the hero of a story. The second person is *you*.

In this lesson, young writers get to experiment with point of view. There is no wrong way to do this, but young writers often skip from first to third person without noticing, and these exercises will help them become aware of where the narrator is in the telling of the story.

Exercise 1: Freewrite

 Freewrite

Write for two minutes without stopping. Don't worry about spelling, grammar or punctuation. If anyone wants to read their freewrite afterwards, they can, but there's no obligation to do so.

Begin with: 'The first/last thing I remember is…'

Exercise 2: Whose story? First, second and third person: which is best?

Writers always have a choice as to who is going to tell their story, and this makes a difference to the story, its tone, voice, style and meaning. This exercise shows how each choice might work.

 Whose story is it exercise

Write an introductory paragraph to a story that begins: 'I spent my early years…'

Then rewrite it in the third person point of view – either: 'He spent his early years…' or: 'She spent her early years…'

Now write it in the second person: 'You spent your early years…'

Here are some examples:

(First person – I)

I was born in a castle on the edge of the Muire River. I lived there until I was twelve, enjoying all the privileges afforded to a young princess. My hair was brushed every morning by servants, and whatever game I wanted to play, servants came to play with me.

(Third person – she)

Princess Jade was born in a castle on the edge of the Muire River. She lived there until she was twelve, enjoying all the privileges afforded to a young princess. Her hair was brushed every morning by servants, and whatever game she wanted to play, servants came to play with her.

(Second person – you)

You were born in a castle on the edge of the Muire River. You lived there until you were twelve, enjoying all the privileges afforded to a young princess. Your hair was brushed every morning by servants, and whatever game you wanted to play, servants came to play with you.

What effect does each point of view have on the reader? Which works best for this piece? Why/why not?

Exercise 3: Drone point of view – the 'everywhere' narrator (or 'omniscient' narrator)

The omniscient (all-knowing) third person point of view is a common way of telling the story where the narrator can move around points of view, like a camera does in a movie. The narrator can look at the wide-angle scene, and then zoom into a tight close-up of someone and then jump immediately into another person's thoughts – finally commenting on these characters. We use the analogy of a drone to show how an omniscient narrator can move about.

✏️ Drone point of view exercise

Create a wide-angle view of a scene (200 words). Zoom in on the scene; describe the setting – the outside and maybe the inside. Then dip into one person's life, showing the reader what they are doing and thinking, and finally, slip next door or outside to another person's (or animal's) life and thoughts. Use the passage below as an example:

The town lay in the shadow of an imposing mountain. Skirting the town was a blue river. The houses that dotted the banks of the river had neat front gardens that looked to be in competition with each other for the amount of flowers and statues that adorned them. It was mid-afternoon and Kylie stood in the middle of Main Street wearing her pyjamas. She had her headphones on and music was blasting at top volume, but no one could hear. She threw her skateboard onto the road and jumped on it. Sure, she knew this was going to draw attention, but she didn't care. In the house just opposite the road, Daisy had already seen her. She called Susan. "Kylie's being weird again," she said. "Go to your window and check it out." It wasn't her nature to be a gossip, but at this point, focusing on someone other than herself was important.

Exercise 4: Telling a story with letters, emails or texts (the epistolary text)

The epistolary text is a story where letters or texts or emails tell the narrative. Lots of famous books use this technique and it can be really exciting, revealing each character from their point of view. Think of texts, diaries and letters from one person to another that might expose secrets, drive the story along and reveal to a reader who the characters are.

✏️ Epistolary exercise

Write a one-page piece using emails, texts, letters or diary entries only. Use the examples below as a jump-off point, or look at previous freewrites for inspiration:

Dear Kylie,

I don't know what's going on or why you are acting strangely, but I thought I should ask. Everyone is talking about it. Last week you skipped volleyball practice and wouldn't return any texts, and now you're out there acting weird in pyjamas. I mean, it's not that weird all by itself, but I don't see the point in not saying anything. Please write back.

Emma

OR:

Dear Diary,

You won't believe what I saw. I've got it all on my phone. I watched the neighbour, Mrs Green, walk into her garden and take out of her bag, a thick wad of hundred-dollar bills. She put them into a Tupperware container and dug a hole in the garden near the fence, burying it! Is this her savings account? I hardly think so. What do I do?

Exercise 5: Getting in tense

The biggest mistake young writers make is switching tense from present to past and vice versa without realising it. This exercise helps them become aware and take control of tenses. It also helps them see which tense works better for any particular piece of writing.

Getting in tense exercise

Write a story in the present tense that begins: 'I get up every morning at six and…'

Then rewrite it in the past tense: 'I got up every morning at six…'

Read the below examples; what is the difference?

Present tense:

Princess Jade lives in a castle on the edge of the Muire River. She enjoys all the privileges afforded to a young princess. Her hair is brushed every morning by servants, and whatever game she wants to play, servants come to play with her.

Past tense:

Princess Jade lived in a castle on the edge of the Muire River. She enjoyed all the privileges afforded to a young princess. Her hair was brushed every morning by servants, and whatever game she wanted to play, servants came to play with her.

Mixed tenses (DO NOT DO!):

Princess Jade lives in a castle on the edge of the Muire River. She enjoyed all the privileges afforded to a young princess. Her hair is brushed every morning by servants, and whatever game she wanted to play, servants come to play with her.

 Extension exercise

Write a 300–500-word piece from a particular point of view. (Choose first, second or third person.) Use one of the exercises from this lesson as a starting point. Decide whether it will take place in the past or present, or even the future. (Ask: which tense is it in?)

Verbal reflection/discussion

What did you enjoy the most in this lesson?

....

....

....

What did you find the most challenging?

....

....

....

....

What new insight or thought about writing did you gain today?

....

....

....

....

Anything else?

....

....

....

....

LESSON 5
IMAGERY

Aim: This lesson sets out to engage young writers in using description and imagery for emotional effect in a narrative piece.

Learning outcomes: By the end of this lesson, young writers will be able to:

- Create impactful writing through sensory description
- Understand and use similes and metaphors to create emotional transportation and amplify meaning

Introduction to lesson

Using the senses is a powerful tool to create setting and establish the mood of a piece. Sensory metaphors and similes can make good writing into great writing. In this lesson, we look at the power of using all five senses to create an unforgettable experience of having been 'there' for the reader. Using figurative language such as similes and metaphors, and extended similes and metaphors (analogies), young writers are shown how to make their observations vivid.

In order to describe a scene, person, event or feeling, use words that create pictures in the reader's mind. We can give a straightforward description: 'the cave was dark and cold and smelly' and use our five senses, but our readers will want to know more – if we found a cave and went inside and told our story, the listener or reader would want to know 'what was it like in there?' Using 'like' (a simile) is inviting the reader to compare the unfamiliar (the cave) to something known ('it was like a fridge!').

Metaphors, too, compare the unfamiliar to something familiar without using 'like', but have the same purpose, and may be stronger than a simile: 'it was a fridge in there!' The exercises in this lesson are designed to show young writers how powerful it can be when the right image or comparison is used. It encourages creativity and sharpens awareness and observation. These exercises will take a bit more time to allow writers to focus on the craft of description.

Exercise 1: Freewrite

 Freewrite

Write for two minutes without stopping. Don't worry about spelling, grammar or punctuation. If anyone wants to read their freewrite afterwards, they can, but there's no obligation to do so.

Begin with: 'All I could see, beyond the sheeting rain, was the glimmer of a flashing light…'

Exercise 2: Sensational senses

Even though everyone knows there are five senses, those most often used in writing are sight and hearing. Young writers often don't think about smell, taste and touch while writing. In the exercise that follows, young writers are asked to think about what it smelled or tasted like. For example, was the inside of the cave cold and damp? Was there a salty taste in the air? Were the walls slimy or rough? Encourage those writing to have fun using all five senses.

 Sensational senses exercise

First, list the five senses: sight, smell, hearing, touch, taste.

Write a short piece, either a poem or a paragraph, with the heading, 'The Cave'. Use all five senses to describe what it is like inside the cave. Is it night or day? Is it winter or summer? Is the mood exciting or scary? What can be seen, smelt, heard, felt, tasted?

Exercise 3: Stunning similes and magnificent metaphors

Similes, as mentioned before, are comparisons between things using the words 'like' or 'as', for example, 'he was as mad as a cut snake', or 'the pelican flew like a jet over the lake'. Metaphors, however, allow for these comparisons without the use of 'like' or 'as', for example, 'that woman is a complete snake', or 'the rain bucketed down'. When young writers engage in using imagery, it's useful to look at some of the examples which show the power of metaphors. In fact, neuroscience shows that when people read unique metaphors involving the senses, for example, 'he had leathery hands', the sensory cortex lights up, whereas if a writer employs ordinary images like 'his hands were rough', the sensory cortex does not light up (Paul, 2012). So, human brains seem to like unique sensory description – and metaphor and simile give young writers the opportunity to do this.

Stunning similes and magnificent metaphors exercise

Write a paragraph like the one below, using the word 'like' comparing things to other things, and then write a second paragraph which does not have to be about the same thing; avoid the word 'like' while still making the comparison.

Here's an example paragraph full of similes:

The heat was like a sticky blanket thrown around my shoulders. It smelled like decay and old clothes with mothballs. The room looked like a set in a bad old movie. And he sat there on his chair like a giant toad.

And here is a paragraph where the similes have been turned to metaphor:

The heat was a sticky blanket thrown around my shoulders. The room was a set in a bad old movie. And he sat there on his chair, a giant toad.

Exercise 4: Catching a kangaroo

An analogy is an extended simile or metaphor. 'Life is like a box of chocolates' is a simile. 'Life is like a box of chocolates – you never know what you're going to get' extends and explains this simile, which would otherwise be obscure.

 Catching a kangaroo exercise

Write a descriptive paragraph comparing a person to an animal. Use either an extended simile or metaphor, or both, exploring all the qualities of that animal as they relate to the person, like the example below. For example, start with this phrase: 'My friend Jenna is a total butterfly…'

Here is an example:

My brother is a mad kangaroo. You'd know this if you've ever tried to catch him. He will leap over fences, clear gates, and if you do get close, his kicks and punches will keep you away. He bounds across the landscape like he has springs in his feet.

 Extension exercise

Expanding on the pieces from this lesson, create a scene of 300–500 words. Engage the senses, and use similes and/or metaphors. Extend some of the similes and metaphors. Make the reader really feel, smell and experience this scene.

Verbal reflection/discussion

What did you enjoy the most in this lesson?

What did you find the most challenging?

What new insight or thought about writing did you gain today?

Anything else?

LESSON 6
SETTING

Aim: This lesson is designed to engage young writers in using the techniques developed for description and imagery to create setting in a narrative piece. It is slower-paced and allows for young writers to spend some time developing their paragraphs in more depth.

Learning outcomes: By the end of this lesson, young writers will be able to:

- Recognise and understand techniques and approaches to create setting in their own and others' work
- Create effective and powerful settings in a narrative piece

Introduction to the lesson

The setting is always important because if there isn't one at the outset of a piece, a reader can feel like the characters are talking in outer space or hanging somewhere until the writer reveals to the reader what and where this is happening. In this lesson, young writers will learn how to create a time and a place and provide the details of the environments that the story happens in, without getting caught up or bogged down by meaningless details. Creating setting is like creating the backdrop to a performance;

some backdrops are highly detailed, and others are simply a wash of colours and suggestions. Both approaches can work.

Exercise 1: Freewrite

 Freewrite

Write for two minutes without stopping. Don't worry about spelling, grammar or punctuation. If anyone wants to read their freewrite aloud afterwards, they can, but there's no obligation to do so.

Begin with: 'As s/he/I looked down from the hilltop at the city below, something shocking caught her/his/my eye…'

Exercise 2: The magic room

 The magic room exercise

Imagine standing in the doorway looking into a magical room. In the room are unfamiliar things, as well as familiar things but used in different ways, or in different forms. Using all five senses and an emotion – wonder, terror, joy, concern, for example – describe what is visible beyond the door in 100–200 words. Is there a trampoline bed? Are the walls painted in different colours or covered in mirrors? Is there a wardrobe on the roof, a tunnel from the window to the sky? There is no limit to what can be imagined – enjoy writing and be as specific as possible so that anyone reading this feels like they are really in that room.

Here is an example:

The door opened into a shimmering cabin-like room. The floor moved and rippled like water, and above there was a ceiling made of mirrors in which the water reflected, confusing everyone at the door. How were we supposed to tell up from down? How could we even trust taking a step onto this shimmering watery floor? At the far end of the room was a bed. The bed was round and covered with blue cushions and it stood, or rather floated, on the floor, the ceiling, its reflection both below and above. Beyond the bed, a wide window let in the light. Trees bent their branches against the glass, framing the view of the expansive gardens that led to purple hills. The scent of perfumed flowers wafted in through the window, smelling both enchanting and sickening at the same time.

Exercise 3: Walking by the river with a million dollars

Setting can be used as a helpful device to mirror what is going on inside the head and heart of the characters. The way setting is described reveals the mood of the character. For example, a forest can seem terrifying or enchanted depending on who is walking in it and what has just happened for them.

 Walking by the river exercise

Imagine how it feels to have just won the lottery – let's say, $50 million! Imagine walking along the banks of a river with this knowledge. Describe the world and how it looks in

200+ words. Don't say anything about the money, just show the reader how it feels. How do the trees look? The sunlight reflecting in the water will have a particular quality. Describe everything from this position of crazy joy – or disbelief. What will this mean for now, for the future?

OR:

Imagine walking by the same river, but something terrible has happened. How does the river look now? What colour are the trees, the sky? Is it winter or summer? Without telling the reader what has happened, show the mood of the character through how the scene is described.

 Extension exercise

Either extend the walking by the river exercise into a longer piece or story, or combine the magic room and walking by the river exercises into a single narrative. Edit and change anything, as necessary.

Verbal reflection/discussion

What did you enjoy the most in this lesson?

What did you find the most challenging?

What new insight or thought about writing did you gain today?

Anything else?

LESSON 7
CHARACTERS

Aim: The purpose of this lesson is to engage young writers in creating characters in a narrative.

Learning outcomes: By the end of this lesson, young writers will be able to:

- Understand how to create compelling characters
- Use techniques such as dialogue, plot and other perceptions to reveal characters and their relationships

Introduction to lesson

A story is not a story without great people in it. Characters drive the plot and the more authentic and relatable they are, the more the reader will care about and want to know what happens to them. To create good characters, young writers need to be aware that each character should have something special about them. It might be a funny moustache, the way they walk, a particular phrase that they say, a view of the world – or all of those. For example, some characters are fearless and will do anything, while some are nervous and will avoid going into difficult situations. It's important to make a character who is compelling and relatable so that readers find themselves invested in following this character through the story.

In the following exercises, young writers are shown how to create believable fictional people.

In helping writers observe people and imagine what it is like to be in their shoes, teachers of writing give them the opportunity to become astute readers of their world, helping them to develop a capacity for empathy as they create characters that may be inspired by real people they have observed in the world around them.

Exercise 1: Freewrite

 Freewrite

Write for two minutes without stopping. Don't worry about spelling, grammar or punctuation. If anyone wants to read their freewrite aloud afterwards, they can, but there's no obligation to do so.

Begin with: 'His face gave it all away in a second...'

Exercise 2: Revealing character through dialogue-driven narrative

Through dialogue, characters show who they are. Dialogue reveals how they speak and what's happening around them. Without the narrator telling the reader about characters, characters can *show* who they are by talking to each other. In this lesson, before they begin, young writers may need to know a few basic rules about how to create dialogue – the important bits relating to form and content.

Here are a few important points for creating good dialogue:

- Use a new line for each speaker and indent the paragraph – unless it's the start of a new chapter or piece, or comes after a big white space, then it's not indented

- Use single quotes in UK and Australia, double in the United States

- Use speech tags to show us who is speaking, when necessary (but don't overuse them; we don't need words like 'he echoed'; 'she exclaimed'; 'he said knowingly...'); keep it simple

- Dialogue should always do these two things: 1) reveal the characters; and 2) move the plot along; each time there is new dialogue or a new speaker, insert a paragraph break (remember, the first paragraph is not indented if it is the beginning of a new piece). Here is an example:

The twins rushed into the kitchen, each one pushing past the other.

'Mum!' Jamie said, 'we've found a real treasure...'

'No, I'm going to tell her,' Rory said. 'We went to the neighbours and discovered a...'

The two faced each other, trying to outshout one another, both talking at once.

'Boys!' Maggie said, stopping them both with a finger to her lips. 'One at a time, please. James, you first and then let Rory tell his part of the story.'

✏ Character-revealing dialogue exercise

Write a dialogue in 5–7 minutes between two characters (for example, a mother and daughter; two animals who speak; a time-traveler and a nine-year-old living today; a brother and a sister walking somewhere). Use only dialogue and no description and no speech tags like 'he said' or 'she said'.

Show:

- Who they are – each character will have a slightly different way of speaking, and a different attitude

Reveal:

- What is going on
- Their relationship to one another
- Their approximate age: kid/teen/adult
- Part of a plot

Here's an example:

'Can you please reconsider, Mum?'

> *'No. I said no more animals in this house until further notice.'*
>
> *'But, Mum…'*
>
> *'Carly, please. We have a zoo here. Why aren't six guinea pigs, two cats and three birds enough…? Wait, what's that you're holding in the bag?'*
>
> *'I couldn't help it. I heard a meowing under the neighbour's car, and I pulled him out. He's tiny. I couldn't leave him there, could I?'*
>
> *'Oh, Carly, he is the cutest thing. What am I supposed to say now?'*

In this example, notice that we haven't used a single speech tag ('she said') because it's obvious who is speaking.

Exercise 3: Character description

Creating a character requires a few fundamental ingredients, such as their name, their appearance, some mannerism they have, some way of speaking. Writers can describe a character or show them through action, or both.

Character description exercise

Describe a character – not every single thing about them, but pick a few things, like the way they talk, what they like to be called, how they walk or something quirky about them. Maybe the character always wears their shirts inside out because they hate the tag scratching against their neck and they don't understand why clothing manufactures would stick tags on the insides of clothing. That would tell you a lot about who this person is.

Here is an example:

Her name was Georgina, but she called herself George. She had short hair, wore her brother's hand-me-down clothes and found herself getting into fights often. Her nails were chewed right down to the skin and her hands were the hands of someone who could fix a broken bike chain no problem or climb over a two-metre gate.

Exercise 4: Speech tags – more dialogue

Speech tags tell the reader how a character said what they said and who said it. It is common for teachers of English and writing to encourage young writers to find as many variations as possible to make the speech tags more interesting in the hope that this makes the conversation more lively. In fact, published writers know that simplifying speech tags, using less of them and keeping them as simple and sparse as possible without losing track of who is speaking, is best. Using punctuation for the desired effect allows the focus to be on the dialogue, which in turn, creates the character.

Speech tags – less is more exercise

Write some more dialogue with only a few speech tags using 'he said', 'she said' only when necessary and ditching all the adverbs such as 'he said knowingly', 'she said adamantly' or 'he exclaimed loudly'.

Here is an example:

> 'I told you before, I don't want to collect clamshells every Saturday!' she screamed exasperatedly.
>
> 'But if you don't, we won't have the money!' he exclaimed annoyingly.

This would be better written as:

> 'I told you before, I don't want to collect clamshells every Saturday,' she said.
>
> 'But if you don't, we won't have the money.'

Write something similar to the two lines above.

Exercise 5: Punctuating dialogue

This exercise helps young writers to put the right punctuation marks in the right places when they are writing dialogue.

 Placing the punctuation in dialogue exercise

Remember:

1. Always start a new paragraph when a new person is speaking.
2. When you open quotes, use single for Australia or the UK, and double for the United States.

3. When you close the quotation marks at the end, the full stop goes inside the quote. If you have 'he said' or 'she said' after the person speaks, there is a comma, not a full stop.

Put the punctuation in the correct places in this dialogue:

You never listen to me he cried

Listen Sam I saw that snake peep out of your shirt collar his mother said You can't take a snake to school with you OK

You don't understand he said He keeps me safe

What are you talking about

He does He peers out if any bullies come near and they just scoot

Placing the punctuation in dialogue answers

'You never listen to me!' he cried.

'Listen, Sam. I saw that snake peep out of your shirt collar,' his mother said. 'You can't take a snake to school with you, OK?'

'You don't understand,' he said. 'He keeps me safe.'

'What are you talking about?'

'He does! He sticks out his head if any bullies come near and they just scoot.'

 Extension exercise

Expand the dialogue pieces into a longer narrative. Add another scene with some description. Drive the story forward with even more dialogue. Decide what each character's biggest fear or biggest hope is and keep that in mind as an underlying motivation for what that character says or does.

CHARACTERS **67**

Verbal reflection/discussion

What did you enjoy the most in this lesson?

What did you find the most challenging?

What new insight or thought about writing did you gain today?

Anything else?

LESSON 8
PURPLE PROSE

Aim: The focus of this lesson is to engage young writers in playing with language and creating 'overwritten' text to discover how sometimes, though not always, 'less is more' in any creative narrative.

Learning outcomes: By the end of this lesson, young writers will be able to:

- Understand when and how 'less is more' in writing practice
- Engage with 'overwriting' and 'lazy writing' to understand how relying on weighty adverbs and adjectives or on clichés can weaken 'voice'

Introduction to lesson

Purple prose can also be called 'overwriting'. It is the result of relying heavily on adjectives and adverbs to convey emotional intensity. But the overuse of these words often weakens writing, makes it sentimental, melodramatic and sometimes even funny. Teachers of English often encourage young writers to use colourful descriptions in order to make their writing more potent. In fact, overwriting is great for comedy, horror or any hyperbole – and it can be made to work in some contexts, but if writers want their work to have pathos and power, then a few well-placed adjectives and adverbs work better than too many.

Exercise 1: Freewrite

 Freewrite

Write for two minutes without stopping. Don't worry about spelling, grammar or punctuation. If anyone wants to read their freewrite aloud afterwards, they can, but there's no obligation to do so.

Begin with: 'She had no sense of time, no sense of direction and no map, but it was impossible to turn back, because…'

Exercise 2: Purple prose

In this exercise, we encourage young writers to overwrite. Create purple prose. Make the writing as sweet, sentimental and overdramatic as possible. The practice of doing the thing we eventually learn how to edit is to deliberately create a piece that may end up looking melodramatic, and then deciding whether that works or not. Encourage the overuse of adjectives!

 Purple prose exercise

Write a paragraph with as many adjectives and adverbs as possible. Think of the paragraph like a chocolate-filled doughnut with too much icing, sprinkles and glazed sugar.

Here's an example:

She walked by the sweet-smelling, exotic, perfumed, delicious rose bushes in her garden, wearing her sequined, beautiful, magical, amazing, white-and-purple frilled dress. Passing by the sucking, sinking, stinking, shaded pond, she tripped on a gnarled, angry, spiky, unruly tree root and slipped into the stinking, messy, muddy marshland at the edge, which seemed to want to suck her down into its ink-dark dripping depths.

Exercise 3: Trimming the fat

 Trimming the fat exercise

Now edit all adverbs, adjectives and unnecessary words out of the piece you just wrote. Simplify it as much as possible. The example below shows the paragraph with almost all the adjectives and adverbs deleted. Sometimes taking out these parts of speech results in writing that is more emotive and powerful.

Our example without purple prose:

She walked by the rose bushes in her garden, wearing her white dress. Passing by the shaded pond, she tripped on a tree root and slipped into the marshland at the edge, which seemed to want to suck her down into its ink-dark depths.

Which piece has more emotional 'punch'? (Answers may vary.)

Exercise 4: Clichés and used-up words

A cliché could be described as an overused metaphor or simile. A cliché is often the first phrase that comes to mind. If I say, 'like water off a...' it is easy to complete the phrase. And if it is easy, it is probably a cliché.

Used-up words are words we use so often they do not mean much – they don't sparkle and make a reader catch their breath. Words like 'nice', 'very', 'kind of', 'sort of' are overused. Being able to spot these lazy words and clichés and replace them can help writing come to life. Alternatively, using them on purpose can be fun.

 Clichés and used-up words exercise

Using the clichés and lazy words below, make a paragraph full of them. Have fun!

Clichés

Like water off a duck's back
As straight as an arrow
As soft as silk
As white as snow
As mad as a cut snake
As flat as a pancake

Lazy words

Nice
Kind of
Sort of
Very

Exercise 5: Vocabulary expansion

The more words young writers have in their toolbox and can use, the more alive they can make their writing. Here's a fun exercise to expand vocabulary.

 Vocabulary expansion exercise

Write a paragraph or two using as many of the below words as possible. Try integrating them seamlessly and naturally, as if they are not part of an exercise!

Luminous
Vacuous
Selected
Distressed
Distant
Problematic
Ominous
Anticipated

 Extension exercise

Using the above exercise as a starting point, write a narrative piece with as few adjectives and adverbs as possible. Edit, rewrite and craft it until it is sharp and powerful.

Verbal reflection/discussion

What did you enjoy the most in this lesson?

What did you find the most challenging?

What new insight or thought about writing did you gain today?

Anything else?

LESSON 9
PLOT AND THE NARRATIVE ARC

Aim: This lesson is designed to engage young writers in understanding the structure of a good plot and how to develop a narrative arc.

Learning outcomes: By the end of this lesson, young writers will be able to:

- Understand and create the most important elements of a good narrative arc

Introduction to lesson

The plot or narrative arc of a story is the map of what happens, when, how and to whom. Every good story has a plot, which usually involves these elements:

1. Somebody wants something
2. Somebody sets out to get something
3. Something stops the person getting what they want, but eventually
4. The person gets what they set out to get

That is the simplest version of a plot, which will be explored in detail in Part B of this book. Perhaps, though, there is only one plot in the world, which is:

Somebody wants something.

In the following exercises, we offer an opportunity for young writers to start thinking about the plot of a story. It's worth noting that writers generally agree that there are 'plotters' and 'pantsers' in the writing world. The 'plotters' map and plot their whole story beforehand, while the 'pantsers' start writing without any idea about where the story is going, allowing the narrative to evolve as they 'write by the seat of their pants'. Neither way is better or worse than the other, and young writers should be encouraged to try both and see what works for them.

Exercise 1: Freewrite

 **Freewrite**

Write for two minutes without stopping. Don't worry about spelling, grammar or punctuation. If anyone wants to read their freewrite aloud afterwards, they can, but there's no obligation to do so.

Begin with: 'I put my hand in my pocket and there it was…'

Exercise 2: Hooking a reader

The 'hook' is the first part of a story, and sometimes even the first sentence that reels the reader in, to use a metaphor. The writer is fishing and has to catch the reader! How do we attract the reader to our bait and make them want to read more? We need to make them curious.

Here is an example of a hook: 'Emma-Jane normally has an explanation for everything, but what she saw on Friday night defied all logic...'

 Hooking a reader exercise

Write a beginning paragraph of about 150 words which has a 'hook' that makes a reader want to read more. (Consider some of the freewrites from previous chapters; maybe one of them is worth using and expanding.)

An example of a 'hook' is any situation where the reader is left wanting to know what might happen next. Think of a story where someone opens a letter that reveals something that shocks the character. The reader wants to know what the character does next.

Exercise 3: A roller-coaster ride

Plot can be seen as a roller-coaster ride. Once a writer sets a story in motion, it will unravel, unfold and shoot forward in that direction. Or, to use another analogy, beginning a narrative is like setting a tiger loose. As long as the tiger leaps forward and doesn't just lie down and curl up, a plot will take a reader on a journey that is hopefully full of unexpected forays into unchartered territories.

 Roller-coaster ride exercise

Take the character from a previous exercise and put them in an impossible situation they cannot get out of… then work to get them out of it! Start with a hook and write a scene that follows in 100–200 words.

Here's an example of a roller-coaster ride story:

Emma-Jane saw the tidal wave coming towards her and for a second, she was paralysed. But then she gathered her most precious possession – her laptop – and her best friend – her cat – and leaped into her car. Just in time. As she drove up the hill, she saw in her rear-view mirror the waves crashing onto her house and smashing it like a matchbox. She raced up the hill, but the waves surged after her... coming closer, faster than she could drive...

By some miracle, the hill grew steep at the very moment the wave would have reached her, and the water crashed white around the mountain, pouring down every side into steep valleys, washing over trees, grasses and rocks, and sinking down in a million thundering waterfalls...

 Extension exercise
Expand and edit one of the exercises.

Verbal reflection/discussion

What did you enjoy the most in this lesson?

What did you find the most challenging?

What new insight or thought about writing did you gain today?

Anything else?

LESSON 10
INNOVATION AND EXPERIMENTATION

Aim: This lesson intends to engage young writers in being creative and innovative, and having the courage to try writing techniques and approaches that may have unexpected outcomes.

Learning outcomes: By the end of this lesson, young writers will be able to:

- Play with techniques and approaches to generate inspiration and ideas
- Understand through writing practice how playing with form can enable conceptual and craft-based innovation

Introduction to lesson

Writing should be a joy. It should be like any other art – a craft and skill that is exciting to work with, allows for creativity, while building skills and capacities. This section allows young writers to take what they've learned and start playing with new ideas – to break away from conformity and to be delighted with what happens.

Exercise 1: Freewrite

 Freewrite

Write for two minutes without stopping. Don't worry about spelling, grammar or punctuation. If anyone wants to read their freewrite aloud afterwards, they can, but there's no obligation to do so.

Begin with: 'I rushed to the door, fighting the wind…'

Exercise 2: Aliens from another universe

A good technique to allow creativity is 'defamiliarisation'. Pretending not to know what a familiar thing is and then writing about it allows for the creation of a fresh perspective.

 Aliens from another universe exercise

Write a passage (100–150 words) of poetry or prose describing to an alien – or any imaginary being – what it is like to be human and to live in a physical body with five senses in this world. Perhaps the alien visitor feels no pain, or doesn't understand emotions, or is so strong that a small touch sends a tow truck flying. Describe to the visitor how it feels to be human, or explain to them what it means to live in this world, noting the alien's different capacities or lack of understanding.

Exercise 3: Magic

Young writers are often confined by what they think is expected of them in their writing – but what if they were given the chance to do absolutely anything with their writing? What if they could experiment with form and content, imagining the wildest things possible, but also play with the visual aspects of their writing to see what meaning can be made when they innovate?

Making magic exercise

Try one of these:

- Do something playful with the words on a page. Look at the poem 'r-p-o-p-h-e-s-s-a-g-r' by E.E. Cummings (overleaf). Look at the way writers use strike-out in a text to show what the narrator wanted to say but isn't saying.
- Play with overlays of one text on top of the other. See the example below by Markus Zusak in *The Book Thief*. Max, a young Jewish man in the story, writes his own story on top of the whited-out pages of Hitler's book against the Jews, *Mein Kampf*.
- Do something not on the list. Push the boundaries of what is expected in terms of words, ideas, form and structure in this exercise. Play. If it looks messy and doesn't make sense, that's fine. It can be long or short. It can be the start of something that will be refined later.

'r-p-o-p-h-e-s-s-a-g-r' by E.E. Cummings

```
                          r-p-o-p-h-e-s-s-a-g-r
                who
a)s w(e loo)k
upnowgath
          PPEGORHRASS
                               eringint(o-
aThe):1
     eA
         !p:
S                                          a
                 (r
rIvInG              .gRrEaPsPhOs)
                                      to
rea(be)rran(com)gi(e)ngly
,grasshopper;
```

The Book Thief by Markus Zusak

Exercise 4: Having fun

Encourage young writers to use their imaginations to see how creative and imaginative they can be with some prompts. They can experiment with either form or content, or both. Importantly, there is certainly no pressure to come up with an amazing product. The purpose is to push the boundaries of what young writers might previously have thought was possible.

 Having fun exercise

Write a short piece with as many of these as possible in it:

- A child's wish
- A goat
- A guide (any kind of guide)
- An apple tree
- A shooting star

Exercise 5: Use what we've done so far

Now it is time to bring all the skills young writers have used and put them together. This will be the focus of Part B, but here is a fun creative way to begin doing this...

 Use what we've done so far exercise

Use at least three of these to write a one-page narrative:

1. Begin with one of the first/second/third person paragraphs previously written

2. Have some dialogue (use 'he said', 'she said' only when needed and incorporate in part, some previous dialogue exercise)
3. Use short sentences to show tension
4. Use a few long sentences of description or when the character is thinking
5. Add a small innovation, either in form or content

Verbal reflection/discussion

What did you enjoy the most in this lesson?

What did you find the most challenging?

What new insight or thought about writing did you gain today?

Anything else?

This is the end of Part A.

Having engaged with exercises that innovate, build voice, character, setting, create melodrama or pathos and elicit empathy in a reader, young writers will now have a host of new writing skills to play with. They have transferable skills that will assist them to express themselves authentically, competently and creatively.

> **Extension/portfolio opportunity**
>
> Expand or edit several pieces from the past 10 lessons, and combine them in a portfolio of work, giving each piece a title. The portfolio should have a title page, and each piece should be on a separate page. Each one of those pieces should have a heading such as: *Short story 'The Pond' written as a result of exercise 5 on page 29.*

If further extension is desired, or if the educator would like a more metacognitive and reflective component to the portfolio, young writers could be requested to add a reflective paragraph on each piece explaining how it was written, what editing was done (show before and after versions of each short piece) and what insights or skills were gained/learned from each included short piece.

The rubric to assess the portfolio is included as Appendix A.

PART B

The hero's journey

INTRODUCTION TO THIS SECTION

Employing the skills learnt in Part A, Part B offers young writers the opportunity to write an extended creative narrative, with a beginning, middle and end. Young writers should now have all the tools they need to launch into Part B.

Each story will be self-edited, peer-edited and teacher-edited to a high standard so that it is publication-ready. In our experience, having a real-world goal like the publication of an anthology leads to a high level of engagement. There are also then opportunities for learning across curriculum areas – such as IT, design, marketing, etc. – but it doesn't have to be that complicated. Having done several anthologies, we've experienced the value for individuals, for groups and for educators in such a goal. We've seen the development of essential and transferable writing skills and we've seen young writers win subsequent writing awards nationally for their work.

The end goal of Part B is to have an anthology that includes all the stories. The editing process is valuable and gives young writers life-long writing skills. Publishing their work helps young writers to understand the purpose and value of good writing. Most of the lessons that follow have minimal instruction, and are designed to allow young writers to *write*. Later, everyone becomes an editor as well as a writer.

There are opportunities for formative and summative assessment along the way throughout Part B. The focus is not on 'correctness' – because authors' styles vary and lots of published authors use 'incorrect' elements like sentence fragments or deliberate omissions – instead, the focus is on control and understanding of language features. The rubrics (Appendix C) we've designed have been tried and tested, and have high inter-rater reliability. Giving feedback using them has been shown to improve writing skills (Carey et al., 2022).

Templates for self-review, peer and teacher feedback and/or assessment are found in Appendices A, B, C and D.

LESSON 11
FINDING A HERO

Aim: The objective of this lesson is to engage young writers in identifying what makes a hero in any narrative. The focus is on character and who will be at the centre of the story. The section expands on ideas presented in Part A when we discussed creating relatable characters.

Learning outcomes: By the end of this lesson, young writers will be able to:

- Create a main character who will be a hero in a narrative
- Understand how a character's need for something drives the story

Introduction to lesson

An anthropologist once set out to try to capture all the stories in the world, from every culture and every time period, to see what these stories had in common. He came to a startling conclusion: there is basically only ONE story all cultures have in common, which he identified as 'the hero's journey'. The man (Joseph Campbell) documented this work in his book *The Hero with a Thousand Faces* (1949). In the hero's journey, someone sets off on a journey to find something or someone, or to achieve or conquer something. Along the way, they face villains or obstacles that threaten to derail the hero from their goal.

Young writers will be given the chance to engage fellow readers using all the skills gained so far to create a story that no one wants to stop reading because readers will become so invested in the hero.

Exercise 1: Freewrite

 Freewrite

Write for two minutes without stopping. Don't worry about spelling, grammar or punctuation. If anyone wants to read their freewrite aloud afterwards, they can, but there's no obligation to do so. This could be the beginning of a longer narrative, you never know…

Begin with: 'The door slammed shut, locking him outside…'

Exercise 2: Someone wants something

The following exercise gives young writers the chance to create a character who may become the hero of their story. This is an exploratory stage and writers can replace their characters or change them down the track, but this is the beginning of the story.

 Someone wants something exercise

Write a summary paragraph about a character who wants something. It can be a thing or a personal goal. What is it? To be a star gymnast/dancer? To work with wild lions? To find a missing twin? Maybe the character wants only one thing, or maybe a few things. Using the example below, write a short paragraph summarising who this person is and what they want.

Sophie (age 11) is adopted. She recently discovered (how?) that she has an identical twin living somewhere in the United States, and she wants to find and meet her. She also wants to find out why they were separated.

Guiding questions:

What does the character Sophie want?

1. To find out where her sister is
2. To find out why they were separated
3. To meet her sister

Exercise 3: Interviewing the hero

 Interviewing the hero – 7 questions exercise

Using the example below, interview the character from the previous exercise. Make up their answers – be spontaneous, funny or sad, or quirky or serious.

1. **Author:** Hi Sophie, as the author of your story, my first question is, what scares you the most?
   Sophie: I'm scared of flying and snakes.

2. **Author:** What are your most embarrassing personal habits?
   Sophie: At night I always run from a distance to jump on my bed in case there are monsters underneath. I also talk in my sleep.

3. **Author:** What foods do you love or hate?
   Sophie: I love hot fries with salt. I hate custard with a passion. It makes me gag.

4. **Author:** What do you want most in the world?
   Sophie: To find my sister. And to find out why we were separated and adopted out to different families in different countries.

5. **Author:** What annoys you the most in other people?
   Sophie: When people say 'all the sudden' instead of 'all of a sudden'. And when they slurp when they drink tea or coffee or soup.

6. **Author:** If you could have dinner with a character from a favourite novel/movie, who would it be and why?
   Sophie: Hermione from Harry Potter. She's smart and funny and brave.

7. **Author:** What keeps you awake at night?
   Sophie: Imagining what happened in the minutes and hours after my sister and I were born.

After answering these questions, there should be a whole treasure chest of ideas and themes that can be part of the story.

Verbal reflection/discussion

What did you enjoy the most in this lesson?

What did you find the most challenging?

What new insight or thought about writing did you gain today?

Anything else?

LESSON 12
(ALMOST) EVERY STORY IS A HERO'S JOURNEY

Aim: This lesson clarifies the essential elements of plot in the 'hero's journey' – and how it emerges from the character's wants and needs.

Learning outcomes: By the end of this lesson, young writers will be able to:

- Plot a story with a beginning, middle and end
- Understand how characters, with their flaws, desires and strengths, move the plot along

Introduction to lesson

Here is the plot structure that underpins the hero's journey:

1. The hero sets out on a journey to reach some goal.
2. The hero has certain powers/gifts/strengths.
3. Along the way, the hero meets a mentor who will help with the quest.
4. The hero will face an enemy or problem which prevents them reaching their goal.

5. The hero uses their powers/gifts/strengths to confront their most difficult challenge.
6. The hero overcomes the problem and reaches the desired goal.

Exercise 1: Freewrite

 Freewrite

Write for two minutes without stopping. Don't worry about spelling, grammar or punctuation. If anyone wants to read their freewrite aloud afterwards, they can, but there's no obligation to do so.

Begin with: 'At night, the wind howled down the mountainside behind our tent …'

Exercise 2: Hero's journeys

The exercise that follows is where most people think we start: plotting. The plot emerges out of the characters' desires, flaws and relationships. All plots need to have a beginning, a middle and an end. The next exercise gives young writers the chance to draw that map broadly.

This series of questions will guide young writers to begin to create the context around their hero's journey.

 Mapping the hero's journey exercise

Write a few brief notes – sentences or paragraphs – in answer to these questions, as this will be the roadmap or the underlying structure of the narrative or story. The answers may evolve, and sometimes it may be challenging to have a definite answer to every one of these questions at this early stage, but give it a go. Answer these questions:

Setting the scene

1. Who is the hero?
2. Where is the hero?
3. Is it day or night?
4. What season?
5. What does it feel like to be there?

The beginning

6. What journey/quest is the hero on?

The middle

7. What problem does the hero face?
8. What powers/gifts/strengths does the hero have?
9. Who is the mentor who will help the hero?

The end

10. What difficult challenge will the hero face
11. What powers/gifts/strengths will they use?
12. How does the hero overcome the problem and reach their goal?

Verbal reflection/discussion

What did you enjoy the most in this lesson?

....

....

....

What did you find the most challenging?

....

....

....

What new insight or thought about writing did you gain today?

....

....

....

Anything else?

....

....

....

LESSON 13
THE ROAD AHEAD...

Aim: This lesson is focused on creating the setting and introducing the hero of the 'hero's journey'.

Learning outcomes: By the end of this lesson, young writers will be able to:

- Write an opening scene that sets a narrative in motion and establishes who the hero is

Introduction to lesson

A story is like a movie. It needs to begin somewhere and the reader needs to be able to imagine this. Using a few beginnings from good YA literature, discuss how a good story starts. It's worth highlighting some of the elements young writers notice in this.

Here is an example...

Read the first two pages of *Harry Potter and the Philosopher's Stone* (Rowling, 1997).

Can these questions be answered:

1. Is it day or night?
2. What season is it?
3. What does it feel like to be there?

And introducing the hero, when Harry is left as a baby on his aunt and uncle's doorstep, can you answer these questions:

1. Who is the hero?
2. Where is the hero?

Give young writers time to look through previous freewrites and anything written in Part A to see if any of these would make a good beginning to their story. It should be clear to them that they can always change any part of the story, but there might be pieces written previously that they want to use.

Exercise 1: Freewrite

 Freewrite

Write for two minutes without stopping. Don't worry about spelling, grammar or punctuation. If anyone wants to read their freewrite aloud afterwards, they can, but there's no obligation to do so.

Begin with: 'The cliff was slippery – there was nothing to hold on to…'

Exercise 2: Setting the scene

 Setting the scene exercise

Using the notes from the last lesson, write an opening scene. It could be a few paragraphs or a whole page – setting the scene. Write without interruption. Use the example and notes for inspiration. Change things if necessary. Play with words and vocabulary. Use metaphors or imagery. Try writing in the first person or the third person. Decide what works best. This might take a whole lesson.

When done, see if the following questions can be answered:

Setting the scene

1. Is it day or night?
2. What season?
3. What does it feel like?
4. Who is the hero?
5. Where is the hero?

Verbal reflection/discussion

What did you enjoy the most in this lesson?

....

....

....

What did you find the most challenging?

....

....

....

What new insight or thought about writing did you gain today?

....

....

....

Anything else?

....

....

....

LESSON 14
THE BEGINNING OF THE HERO'S JOURNEY

Aim: This lesson is focused on creating the beginning of the story.

Learning outcomes: By the end of this lesson, young writers will be able to:

- Write an inception or precipitating event that starts the hero off on their quest

Introduction to lesson

In the beginning of a story, young writers need to focus on their protagonist and show some of their weaknesses, doubts and fears as well as what the hero is after. They can draw on their own experiences. They can think about any feelings they've ever had about not being fast/good/brave/smart/strong enough to manage what was in front of them, or draw on any times they've ever thought, 'I just have to do this, regardless of the outcome.' They should think about the dialogue exercise and write some dialogue. Encourage them to use short sentences to create tension, and to not forget about description, metaphors, similes and everything they've experimented with so far.

Exercise 1: Freewrite

 Freewrite

Write for two minutes without stopping. Don't worry about spelling, grammar or punctuation. If anyone wants to read their freewrite aloud afterwards, they can, but there's no obligation to do so.

Begin with: 'The last words he said before he vanished were…'

Exercise 2: The beginning

 The beginning exercise

Write a few paragraphs that show the reader what the hero wants. There might be an event that sets the hero off on their journey. Describe that. Fall into the story now and get lost in it.

When done, is it possible to answer the question: What journey/quest is the hero on?

Verbal reflection/discussion

What did you enjoy the most in this lesson?

What did you find the most challenging?

What new insight or thought about writing did you gain today?

Anything else?

LESSON 15
ON THE JOURNEY – FUN AND GAMES

Aim: This lesson is focused on building the middle of the story, where all the 'fun 'n' games' happen.

Learning outcomes: By the end of this lesson, young writers will be able to:

- Write the middle part of the story using many of the skills and capacities from previous lessons

Introduction to lesson

In the middle of a story, young writers are invited to be 'pantsers' – writing by the seat of their pants. They've done all the plotting, so they have the scaffolding they need. Now it's time for what screenwriters sometimes call 'fun 'n' games'. This is where the hero faces a problem and has to call on unique powers, gifts and strengths. It's also the time when the hero meets the mentor or guide who offers assistance. Remind young writers that if the story starts going off in a direction they didn't plan, to go with it. This is often where the magic happens.

Exercise 1: Freewrite

 Freewrite

Write for two minutes without stopping. Don't worry about spelling, grammar or punctuation. If anyone wants to read their freewrite aloud afterwards, they can, but there's no obligation to do so.

Begin with: 'Someone watched the camp from the ridge…'

Exercise 2: The middle – fun 'n' games

 The middle – fun 'n' games exercise

This is where writing gets more exciting and sometimes even goes in directions writers don't expect. Don't worry if this happens. Sometimes the best storytelling happens this way.

Write one to three pages where the hero faces a problem, has to use a gift or strength and maybe meets a mentor or another character who can help.

When done, can these questions be answered:

1. What problem does the hero face?
2. What powers/gifts/strengths does the hero have?
3. Who is the mentor/character who will help the hero?

Verbal reflection/discussion

What did you enjoy the most in this lesson?

What did you find the most challenging?

What new insight or thought about writing did you gain today?

Anything else?

LESSON 16
THE ENDING – ALL IS (NOT) LOST

Aim: This lesson is focused on concluding the story.

Learning outcomes: By the end of this lesson, young writers will be able to:

- Write a fitting conclusion to a narrative that ties up all loose ends and resolves the story

Introduction to lesson

As a story draws to a close, young writers need to know that there's usually an 'all is lost' moment, which is the exact opposite of the ending. In this moment before the real end, it looks like the hero's struggle has been for nothing. For example, if Sophie is looking for her twin sister, there would be a moment when it would look like all her efforts have come to nothing. This makes the ending all the more powerful when things *do* tie up. Tying things up can be challenging, but also fun. We suggest that, if they wish, young writers discuss their stories with a peer before moving on to the next exercise, to get feedback and thoughts on their resolution.

Exercise 1: Freewrite

 Freewrite

Write for two minutes without stopping. Don't worry about spelling, grammar or punctuation. If anyone wants to read their freewrite aloud afterwards, they can, but there's no obligation to do so.

Begin with: 'A bang, like a balloon popping, rang through the air…'

Exercise 2: The ending

 The ending – all is (not) lost exercise

Write an 'all is lost' scene. In this part, it looks like the hero will not make it. Then move the story to its resolution. Finally, the hero gets what they set out to find/achieve.

When done, can these questions be answered:

1. What final difficult challenge will your hero face; what is the 'all is lost' moment?
2. What powers/gifts/strengths will they use?
3. How does the hero overcome the problem and reach their goal?

Verbal reflection/discussion

What did you enjoy the most in this lesson?

What did you find the most challenging?

What new insight or thought about writing did you gain today?

Anything else?

LESSON 17
EDITING THE STORY

Aim: The purpose of this lesson is to engage young writers in a thorough self-editing process using the self- and peer-editing rubric (Appendix C).

Learning outcomes: By the end of this lesson, young writers will be able to:

- Recognise techniques and approaches in their own work and edit with awareness
- Evaluate their own work
- Through editing, develop transferable literacy capacity
- Improve communication on techniques and approaches in own work

Introduction to lesson

Stephen King suggested that there are two stages to writing a story: firstly, the writer writes with the door closed (Strobey, 1991). This means, writers write without anyone else reading their work. Once that writing is done, it is time to open the door and let others read it and give feedback. Writing with the door open means editing the story for others' eyes. There are two types of editing that will be applied to the stories that have been written:

1. **Structural editing** – this involves looking for errors in meaning. Young writers can ask themselves if everything is clear in the story and whether it all makes sense and holds together. Structural editing focuses on *flow* and *content*.
2. **Copy editing** – this comes after structural editing. This involves looking for grammatical errors: punctuation, spelling, sentence structure, etc. and focuses on *form*.

The edit (regardless of whose story it is) is to make the story the best it can be. Good editors have to also be sensitive to writers, recognising that they have poured their hearts into the work. When editing, highlight what is working, as well as what isn't working and why. Use the common spelling errors provided below as a helpful checklist.

Common spelling errors

Here is a checklist that you can use as a start for editing your or anyone else's work to make sure these common words are being used correctly:

1. its/it's
2. weather/whether
3. there/their/they're
4. your/you're
5. which/witch
6. wear/where/were
7. past/passed

Exercise 1: Copy-editing practice

 Copy-editing exercise

Working with a peer, edit this paragraph. Use the common spelling errors list as a start. When you're done, check against Version 2 below, where the errors have been corrected.

Version 1

Rain bucketed down and Daisy could bearly see out of the window the bus stopped at school and the doors opened they're was the smell of rain on hot tarmac Queensland in the summer could be baking by eight in the morning in January. Daisy Walker was sick and tired of all the jokes. They where jokes for the bunch of idiots at the back of the bus but not for her. Today would be different. Today things would change. Nobody knew what she had in her pocket. She didn't know when she was going to use it, but at some point she definitely was. Their was nothing anyone could do about it she got off the bus hey lazy Daisy, Jarrod said he was as thick as a brick she thought so why did he annoy her so much? She wondered weather she would be able to hold out long enough to execute her plan but then she had nothing to lose and everything to gain. Your going to regret this Daisy said calmly I don't think so, said Jarrod. I never have and I never well. Its time you learned a lesson Jarrod Daisy said.

Version 2

Rain bucketed down and Daisy could <u>barely</u> see out of the window<u>.</u> The bus stopped at school and the doors opened<u>. There</u> was the smell of rain on hot tarmac<u>.</u> Queensland in the summer could be baking by eight in the morning in January. Daisy Walker was sick and tired of all the jokes. They <u>were</u> jokes for the bunch of idiots at the back of the bus<u>,</u> but not for her. Today would be *different. Today things would change. Nobody knew what she had in her pocket. She didn't know when she was going to use it, but at some point she definitely was. There was nothing anyone could do about it. She got off the bus.*

'Hey, lazy Daisy,' Jarrod said. He was as thick as a brick, she thought, so why did he annoy her so much? She wondered whether she would be able to hold out long enough to execute her plan, but then she had nothing to lose and everything to gain.

'You're going to regret this,' Daisy said calmly.

'I don't think so,' said Jarrod. 'I never have and I never will.'

'It's time you learned a lesson, Jarrod,' Daisy said.

Using all the skills learned in Part A, young writers can take the self-review template (Appendix C) as an editing guide on their own stories. They can make comments in the boxes. They should be given enough time to do this thoroughly and not feel rushed.

For the next lesson, young writers will need to have their rewritten clean draft in hard copy as it's to be used in the classroom.

Exercise 2: Self-editing exercise

 Self-editing exercise

This self-edit is a sculpting and shaping exercise. Enjoy this part.

Using the self-editing template (Appendix C), read through your story. This is the time to add metaphors, delete too many adjectives and use fragments. Use short sentences. Use long sentences. Tweak dialogue. Have fun reworking the story. Make any changes. Rewrite any sections as much or as little as you see fit. Take the story home and work on it if you run out of time.

Verbal reflection/discussion

What did you enjoy the most in this lesson?

....
....
....

What did you find the most challenging?

....
....
....
....

What new insight or thought about writing did you gain today?

....
....
....
....

Anything else?

....
....
....
....

LESSON 18
PEER EDITING

Aim: This lesson seeks to engage young writers in a thorough peer-editing process using the rubric (Appendix C).

Learning outcomes: By the end of this lesson, young writers will be able to:

- Recognise techniques and approaches in others' work
- Evaluate other writers' work
- Improve communication relating to techniques and approaches in others' work

Introduction to lesson

In this lesson, young writers will apply their editing skills to someone else's work. We suggest that the teacher/educator takes in all stories and then randomly redistributes these to others. Each student then receives a random story to edit. Obviously, no one should receive their own story!

Exercise 1: Applying editing skills to others' work

The peer edit is exactly like the self-edit. Editing another's work is a great way to get on top of all elements of writing. Young writers should be encouraged to say helpful and thoughtful things in the comment boxes if they do make any comments.

 Peer-editing exercise

This peer edit is a helpful exercise designed to assist another writer to make their story the best it can be. Using the peer-editing template (Appendix C), which is exactly the same as the self-editing one, read through a peer's story and respond to each element. The aim is to help that story *be as true to itself as it can be*. This requires trying to see what the writer of that story wants that story to be.

Once young writers receive their drafts back, they should be reminded that the feedback is simply that – feedback. They can use what is useful, and discard what isn't. Whatever improves the work, in their now-informed opinion, is worthwhile, and if they don't agree with the feedback, they can be free not to use it.

Verbal reflection/discussion

What did you enjoy the most in this lesson?

What did you find the most challenging?

What new insight or thought about writing did you gain today?

Anything else?

LESSON 19
FINAL EDIT

Aim: This lesson is designed to engage young writers in a final edit of their work, taking into account specific feedback based on the rubric (Appendix C).

Learning outcomes: By the end of this lesson, young writers will be able to:

- Apply feedback to a reworking of their narrative

Exercise 1: Final edit

In this lesson, young writers will complete their final edit on their story. Considering feedback from their peer editors, they can fine-tune their story and work on a semi-final draft which will then be handed in to the teacher for assessment and final edits.

Teachers/educators can assess and mark the stories against the rubric. Young writers then edit their final story according to teacher feedback. This can be the end of the project, or the stories can be collected for an anthology and a book launch at the end of the process.

Verbal reflection/discussion

What did you enjoy the most in this lesson?

What did you find the most challenging?

What new insight or thought about writing did you gain today?

Anything else?

LESSON 20
IN-CLASS SHOWCASE

Aim: This lesson intends to engage young writers in a final presentation and reading of their work to their peers.

Learning outcomes: By the end of this lesson, young writers will be able to:

- Communicate through reading and sharing a narrative extract to their peers

Introduction to lesson

In this lesson, young writers will showcase their accomplishment by reading a part of their story to the class (one page per person, or one to two minutes each), and no pressure if someone doesn't wish to read. There is no requirement for feedback, but teachers may comment and point to an element or two that stood out in each reading.

Creating an anthology and having a book launch

Objective: To publish and share a cleanly edited anthology of young writers' work.

At the end of the launch, young writers should come away from the project feeling:

- Respected, valued, supported and connected
- Proud of their identity as an author

Creating the anthology

Follow these steps to create the anthology:

1. Ask the young writers to suggest a title that captures the themes of the stories.
2. Decide how many stories/poems are going to be included.
3. Ask the young writers to choose their best or favourite story.
4. Decide on what order you want the stories to be.
5. Decide on who will write an introduction – maybe the teacher.
6. Find a designer to format and design the anthology, and decide whether you want illustrations, white space, etc. (Maybe a parent?)
7. Publish the anthology – either online or printed copies, or both. Blurb and Amazon offer options that we have used and found intuitive and not too arduous. Conduct research to find the best option, and allow for lead time as orders can take up to six weeks to arrive.
8. Launch the anthology – invite friends, family and relevant people in the community. The launch may take place a couple of months down the track – publishing is not a fast process.

Book a launch

We believe that having a book launch is an important capstone experience of the *Write Now!* program.

Things to consider

1. **Timing**
   - Get an estimate date of the arrival of books from the publisher (if you use a print-on-demand service like Amazon) and leave time for unexpected delays. When is the best time most parents and families will be able to attend?

2. **Location**
   - Where will the book launch take place?
   - Does space need to be booked?

3. **Music**
   - Consider having a school band or orchestra providing music to integrate the talents of others.

4. **Invitees**
   - Look into having personalised invitations for parents of the authors.
   - Contemplate involving special guests, such as a local author or a friendly mayor, to the launch to showcase the young writers and the school within the community.
   - Invite the local media.

5. **Book reading**
   - Include a reading of about 45 minutes where the young authors each read a minute or two of their work as they did for their classmates.

6. **Sales**
   - Consider sales at the launch. Proceeds from sales can reimburse the initial outlay, and after that, the class could decide what to do with any additional funds – or this could contribute to next year's anthology. Perhaps proceeds could cover a free book for each author.

7. **Library**
   - Consider having a copy of the book in the school library.

Verbal reflection/discussion

What did you enjoy the most in this lesson?

What did you find the most challenging?

What new insight or thought about writing did you gain today?

Anything else?

REFERENCES

Anderson, L.W., & Krathwohl, D.R. (Eds.). (2001). *A Taxonomy for Learning, Teaching, and Assessing: A Revision of Bloom's Taxonomy of Educational Objectives*. New York: Longman.

Australian Curriculum. (2021). Critical and Creative Thinking. www.australiancurriculum.edu.au/f-10-curriculum/general-capabilities/critical-and-creative-thinking

Beers, K. (2003). *When Kids Can't Read: What Teachers Can Do*. Portsmouth, NH: Heinemann. Retrieved from http://middlesecondarytoolkit.pbworks.com/f/mainidea111509.pdf

Braine, J. (1975). *Writing a Novel*. London: McGraw-Hill.

Brolin, C. (1992). 'Kreativitet och Kritiskt tandande. Redsckap for framtidsberedskap' ('Creativity and critical thinking. Tools for preparedness for the future'), in *Krut*, 53, 64–71.

Carey, M.D., Davidow, S., & Williams, P. (2022). Re-imagining narrative writing and assessment: a post-NAPLAN craft-based rubric for creative writing. *The Australian Journal of Language and Literacy, 45*(9).

Carver, R. (1981). A Storyteller's Shoptalk. *The New York Times* [online], 15 February. https://archive.nytimes.com/www.nytimes.com/books/01/01/21/specials/carver-shoptalk.html?_r=1&oref=slogin

Cliatt, M., Puckett, M.J., & Shaw, J.M. (1988). The Storytime Exchange: Ways to Enhance It. *Childhood Education, 64*(5), 293–298. (ERIC Document Reproduction Service No. EJ373896.)

Cummings, E.E. (2016). *E.E. Cummings: Complete Poems, 1904–1962*, George James Firmage (Ed). Liveright; 1st edition (12 August).

Davidow, S., & Cunnane, M. (2014). Mixing literacy with innovation. *Teacher Magazine.* www.teachermagazine.com/au_en/articles/mixing-literacy-with-innovation

Davidow, S,. & Williams, P. (2016). *Playing with Words: An Introduction to Creative Writing Craft.* Bloomsbury.

Dillard, A. (1981). Contemporary Prose Styles. *Twentieth Century Literature, 27*(23), 207–222.

Dweck, C. (2015). Growth Mindset, Revisited. *Education Week, 35*(05), 23 September.

Eder, D.J. (2007). Bringing Navajo Storytelling Practices into Schools: The Importance of Maintaining Cultural Integrity. *Anthropology & Education Quarterly, 38*(3), 278–296.

Elbow, P. (1973). *Writing without Teachers.* New York: Oxford University Press.

Franklin, J., & Theall, M. (2021). Developing creative capacities. *Idea.* www.ideaedu.org/idea-notes-on-learning/developing-creative-capacities/

Gibson, S. (2008). Reading aloud: A useful learning tool? *ELT Journal, 62* (1), 29–36.

Gonzalez, J. (2018). Moving from Feedback to Feedforward. *Cult of Pedagogy*, 21 January. www.cultofpedagogy.com/feedforward

Goodwin, P., & Redfern, A. (2000). *Reading aloud to children.* Reading: University of Reading, Reading Language and Information Centre.

Hirsch, J. (2017). *The Feedback Fix: Dump the Past, Embrace the Future, and Lead the Way to Change.* London: Rowman & Littlefield Publishers.

Isbell, R., Sobol, J., Lindauer, L., & Lowrance, A. (2004). The Effects of Storytelling and Story Reading on the Oral Language Complexity and Story Comprehension of Young Children. *Early Childhood Education Journal, 32*(3), 157–163.

Le Guin, U.K. (1998). *Steering the Craft: Exercises and Discussions on Story Writing for the Lone Navigator or the Mutinous Crew.* Portland: Eighth Mountain Press.

Lodge, D. (1992). *The Art of Fiction.* London: Vintage.

Mello, R. (2001). Building Bridges: How Storytelling Influences Teacher/Student Relationships. (ERIC Document Reproduction Service No. ED457088.)

Miller, S., & Pennycuff, L. (2008). The Power of Story: Using Storytelling to Improve Literacy Learning. Journal of Cross-Disciplinary Perspectives in Education, *1*(1), 36–43.

Orwell, G. (1946). *Politics and the English Language.* London: Penguin. www.orwell.ru/library/essays/politics/english/e_polit

Paul, A.M. (2012). Your Brain on Fiction. *The New York Times.* 17 March. www.nytimes.com/2012/03/18/opinion/sunday/the-neuroscience-of-your-brain-on-fiction.html#

Rowling, J.K. (1997). *Harry Potter and the Philosopher's Stone.* London: Bloomsbury.

Strobey, W. (1991). Digging up stories with Stephen King. Interview by Wallace Strobey. *Writer's Digest*, 16 September. http://wallacestroby.com/writersonwriting_king.html

Strunk, W., & White, E.B. (1918). *The Elements of Style.* (First British printing: 1 July 1997, Bloomsbury Books.) Essex: Pearson Education Limited.

Wallace, C. (2000). Storytelling: Reclaiming an Age-Old Wisdom for the Composition Classroom. *Teaching English in the Two-Year College, 27*(4), 434–439.

Williams, P. (2016). Teaching bad writing. *New Writing: The International Journal for the Practice and Theory of Creative Writing, 13*(3), 368–377.

Williams, P. (2017). Playing with Words: Encouraging Failure in the First Year. *Writing in Education, 71*(2), 67–71.

Zusak, M. (2007). *The Book Thief.* Alfred A. Knopf.

NOTE ON RUBRICS AND ASSESSMENT OF CREATIVE WRITING

The rubrics provide opportunities for dialogue and interaction. The criteria are designed to be learning tools – assessment-as-learning. In this feedback process, young writers engage with a more fluid assessment model based on the imaginative capacities of the writer and aspects of control rather than 'doing it right'.

This scale on the rubric corresponds to the conventional A–F scale (emerging: E–F; competent: C–D; sophisticated: A–B), but in the spirit of feeding forward, the language is more appropriate for a draft where further work can help improve the writing. Connotatively, 'emerging', for example, implies encouragement, whereas 'fail' or 'E' implies summative finality.

Should teachers not wish to provide a letter grade for the final story, rubrics can be used without adding points. It works just as well to provide feedback on the criteria without assigning scores or using smiley faces to indicate how competently the editor or educator believes certain criteria have been met. Finally, we offer a course-feedback template so that educators can discover how young writers believe the program has benefitted them. As authors, we have found this particularly inspiring and illuminating.

Write Now – there's never been a better time!

APPENDIX A
PORTFOLIO MARKING TEMPLATE – SELF-REVIEW

Portfolio submission for the end of Part A

Select five pieces to submit for assessment. Minimum 500 words; maximum 1,000 words.

These may include paragraphs, poetry, descriptive pieces or any of the exercises completed in class or for homework.

Young writers should ensure each piece has a heading and the title of the exercise it is illustrating, for example: 'Raindrops – run-on-sentence exercise'. Writers should use the portfolio marking template to first read their own work, then one other person's work, giving feedback, before submitting a final draft to a teacher.

Self- and peer-review for portfolio

No.	The pieces in this portfolio…	☺	☺☺	☺☺☺	Comments
1	Have original ideas				
2	Are well-structured				
3	Use short and long sentences				
4	Use fragments, run-ons or other devices for effect				

No.	The pieces in this portfolio…	☺	☺☺	☺☺☺	Comments
5	Use strong imagery, metaphors or similes				
6	Use the five senses in description				
7	Use overwriting, lazy writing or minimalism on purpose				
8	Use the tenses correctly				
9	Show control of grammar and punctuation				
10	Are free of unintentional spelling errors				

(Three smiley faces = excellent)

APPENDIX B
PORTFOLIO MARKING TEMPLATE – EDUCATOR

Educator review of portfolio

The headings refer to the capacity of the young writer: emerging = can only do at a very basic level; competent = can use devices consciously; and sophisticated = the capacity is native and amazing things result!

No.	The pieces in this portfolio…	Emerging 0–3	Competent 4–7	Sophisticated 8–10	Comments
1	Have original ideas				
2	Are well-structured				
3	Use short and long sentences				
4	Use fragments, run-ons or other devices for effect				
5	Use strong imagery, metaphors or similes				
6	Use the five senses in description				

No.	The pieces in this portfolio…	Emerging 0–3	Competent 4–7	Sophisticated 8–10	Comments
7	Use overwriting, lazy writing or minimalism on purpose				
8	Use the tenses correctly				
9	Show control of grammar and punctuation				
10	Are free of unintentional spelling errors				
Total					/100

APPENDIX C
STORY MARKING TEMPLATE

Author: _____

Story title: _____

Marker: ☐ Self   ☐ Teacher   ☐ Peer

No.	Item	Emerging 1 ☺	Competent 2–3 ☺☺	Sophisticated 4–5 ☺☺☺	Total /100	Comments
CREATIVITY AND INNOVATION						
This story…						
1	is an original idea either in the content or in the way it is structured					
2	readability – creates interest in the character and the plot					
THE PLOT						
This story…						
3	follows the structure of the hero's journey					
4	has a beginning that hooks readers					

No.	Item	Emerging 1 ☺	Competent 2–3 ☺☺	Sophisticated 4–5 ☺☺☺	Total /100	Comments
5	has a complication or conflict that keeps you reading					
6	ends with a satisfying resolution					
WORDS AND SENTENCES						
This story…						
7	includes short and long sentences					
8	includes fragments/ run-ons or other devices for effect					
9	includes imagery, metaphors or similes					
10	engages the five senses in description					
11	is free of overwriting or lazy writing					
12	uses tenses correctly					
CHARACTERS, CONTEXT AND DIALOGUE						
In this story…						
13	the setting is clear					
14	dialogue moves the plot along and reveals the characters					

No.	Item	Emerging 1 ☺	Competent 2-3 ☺☺	Sophisticated 4-5 ☺☺☺	Total /100	Comments
15	a few key descriptions make the characters unique					
16	there is control of point of view: first – I; second – you; third – he/she/they					

STRUCTURAL ELEMENTS AND PRESENTATION

In this story…

No.	Item	Emerging	Competent	Sophisticated	Total	Comments
17	paragraphs are spaced consistently					
18	there is control of dialogue formatting					
19	there is control of grammar and punctuation					
20	the writing is free of spelling errors					
TOTAL SCORE						

APPENDIX D
YOUNG AUTHORS' RESPONSE TO THE PROGRAM

Author: _____

Feedback review questions	Responses (Note: there are no right or wrong answers)
What did you find helpful that you feel has impacted your writing the most?	
What did you find most challenging in the whole course?	
What did you enjoy the most?	
Any other comments?	

www.ingramcontent.com/pod-product-compliance
Lightning Source LLC
Chambersburg PA
CBHW050240120526
44590CB00016B/2168